In The Home

Kath Cox and Pat Hughes

Wayland

HISTORY FROM PHOTOGRAPHS ·

Notes for Parents and Teachers

This book provides a flexible teaching resource for Early Years history. Two levels of text are given – a simple version and a more advanced and extended level. The book can be used for:

◆ Early stage readers at Key Stage 1
◆ Older readers needing differentiated text
◆ Non-readers who can use the photographs
◆ Extending skills of reading non-fiction
◆ Adults reading aloud to provide a model for non-fiction reading

By comparing photographs from the past and the present, children are able to develop skills of observation, ask questions and discuss ideas. They should begin by identifying the familiar in the modern photographs before moving on to the photographs from the past. The aim is to encourage children to make 'now' and 'then' comparisons.

The use of old photographs not only provides an exciting primary resource for history but, used alongside the modern photographs, aids the discussion of the development of photography. Modern photographs in black and white are included to encourage children to look more closely at the photographs and avoid seeing the past as 'black and white'. All the historical photographs were taken beyond the living memory of children and most have been selected from the Edwardian period between 1900–1920. A comprehensive information section for teachers, parents and other adults on pages 29–31 gives details of each of the old photographs, where known, and suggests points to explore and questions to ask children.

Editors: Dereen Taylor and Joanna Bentley
Designer: Michael Leaman
Production Controller: Carol Stevens
Consultant: Suzanne Wenman

Front cover: The main photograph is of women at leisure in the home, 1912. The inset photograph is of a family at leisure in the home.
Endpapers: Photographers at work at a wedding, 1907.
Title page: Children photographed on the steps of their home, c.1900.

Picture Acknowledgements
The publishers would like to thank the following for allowing their pictures to be used in this book: Beamish, The North of England Open Air Museum 7, 13, 17; Angus Blackburn **cover inset**; Mary Evans Picture Library title page, 11; Hulton Deutsch Collection 15, 25; Impact Photos Ltd 26; Tizzie Knowles 4, 6, 8, 10, 12, 14, 16, 18, 20, 22, 24; Billie Love Historical Collection 5, 23; Public Record Office of Northern Ireland **cover main**; Popperfoto 9; Royal Photographic Society contents page, endpapers; Rural History Centre, University of Reading 27; Tameside Local Studies Library 21 (inset); Topham Picture Source 19.

First published in 1996 by Wayland (Publishers) Limited
61 Western Road, Hove, East Sussex BN3 1JD, England

© Copyright 1996 Wayland (Publishers) Limited

The right of Kath Cox and Pat Hughes to be identified as the authors of this work has been asserted in accordance with the Copyright, Designs and Patents Act 1988.

British Library Cataloguing in Publication Data
Cox, Kath
School. – (History from Photographs Series)
I. Title II. Hughes, Pat III. Series
371.009

ISBN 0-7502-1542-9

Typeset in the UK by Michael Leaman Design Partnership
Printed and bound in Great Britain by B.P.C. Paulton Books Ltd

• Contents •

A Brownie box camera and case, 1900

Some of the more difficult words appear in the text in **bold**.
These words are explained in the picture glossary on page 28.
The pictures will help you to understand the entries more easily.

The Arif family live in this house.

Their home has three rooms downstairs and four rooms upstairs.
There is a garage for the car and a garden to play in.
Water, gas and electricity come into the house through
underground pipes and cables.

These children had their photograph taken outside their home.

Houses like this usually had four rooms.
There was a **parlour** and kitchen downstairs with two bedrooms upstairs.
Few homes had gas or electricity.
Many homes did not have water piped into the house.

This kitchen is bright and easy to keep clean.

Crockery, **utensils** and food are stored in cupboards on the walls.
Food is prepared on **worktops**.
A washing machine, dishwasher and other kitchen appliances make
many jobs in the home quicker and easier.

The coal fire made this kitchen harder to keep clean.

Families had fewer goods to store so they did not need
as many kitchen cupboards.
Most meals were home-made using fresh food bought each day.
Women did most work in the home by hand.
There were few machines to help them.

Mr Nasim is putting a dish of food in the oven.

Most homes have a gas or electric oven.

Ovens like this are easy to use and to keep clean.

The temperature is controlled by a knob or button.

Most modern ovens are only used to cook food.

Most homes had a range in the kitchen.

A coal fire inside the range gave out heat.

This made the temperature hard to control.

The range was used for cooking food and heating water.

Cleaning the range was very hard work because it was made of cast iron.

Mrs Benn washes clothes in a washing machine.

The machine fills with water and heats it to the right temperature. It washes and rinses the clothes. Then the water is drained and the clothes spun dry. Many clothes can be washed in a short time.

Washing clothes was hard work.

Clothes were
washed by hand
in the **scullery**
or outside.
Water was heated
in a **copper** over
a fire.
A **dolly** was
used to get the
dirt out of
the clothes.
The washing was
rinsed and
squeezed through
a **mangle**.

Jenny irons her clothes with an electric iron.

Modern irons are light and easy to use because
they are made from plastic and metal.
The right temperature can be set for different cloth.

Many women used a flat iron.

Flat irons were made of solid metal.
They had to be heated by the fire or on the kitchen range.
There was no way to control the iron's heat.
Ironing was very hard work.

Sarah is cleaning the house.

Today homes are easy to keep clean.
Gas fires and electric lights do not make dust or **soot**.
Vacuum cleaners and special sprays and polishes
make cleaning quick and easy.

Only rich families had a vacuum cleaner.

In most homes women cleaned using a dustpan and brush.
Soot and dust from coal fires and gas lights made houses dirty.
Furniture and floors had to be dusted, scrubbed and polished
to keep them clean.

Jamie and Martin have a bath every night before bedtime.

Hot and cold water is piped to the taps.
The family can also wash their hands and face in a sink.

Many homes did not have a bathroom.

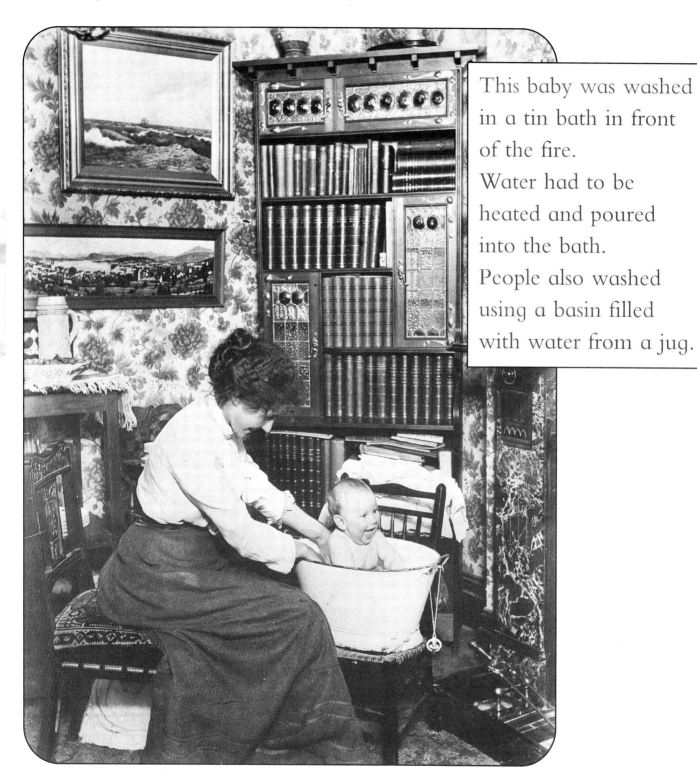

This baby was washed in a tin bath in front of the fire.
Water had to be heated and poured into the bath.
People also washed using a basin filled with water from a jug.

The toilet is inside the house.

Toilets are made in many different colours.

Clean water from the **cistern** flushes the toilet after it is used.

Modern toilets are clean and hygienic.

Many homes had the toilet outside.

The toilet was in a small building in the yard.
There was no running water so ashes were put in the toilet after it was used.
Newspaper and scrap paper were used as toilet paper.

Toby has his own bedroom.

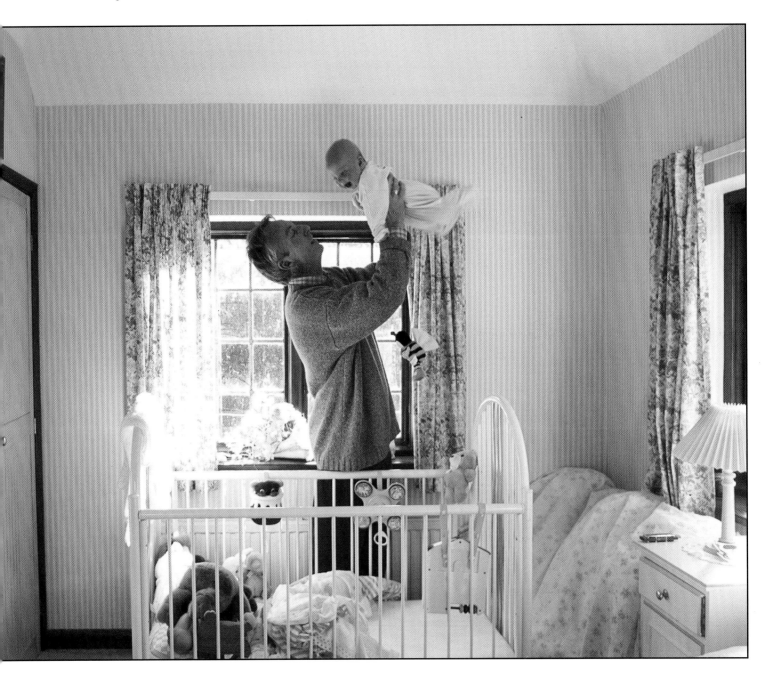

He sleeps in a cot.

Light colours on the walls and ceiling make the room bright.

There are two other bedrooms in this house.

This baby slept in a wooden crib.

In rich families children slept in a nursery
with a nanny to look after them.
In poorer homes the children shared one room
or slept in their parents' bedroom.

Chris likes to read in the living room.

Sometimes Chris listens to music or watches television.
She spends a lot of time in this room.
It is a bright, comfortable room.

This room was called the drawing room.

In larger homes wealthy families used the drawing room in the evenings.
They read, talked, sang or played musical instruments.
In smaller homes the parlour was used only for visitors or special occasions.

The Evans family like to spend time in their living room.

It is a warm and comfortable room.
The children have space to play while their parents watch television.

The kitchen was the most important room in this home.

The range kept the kitchen warm.

Children and parents ate their meals here.

Families spent the evenings sitting in the kitchen.

Kathy does her homework each night.

Kathy's mum works too. She works from home using her computer and the telephone. Today many people do paid work from home.

This family made small toys in their home.

In some families only women worked from home.
In the poorest families the children had to help too.
Sewing, washing and making brushes are examples
of paid work done in the home.

· Picture Glossary ·

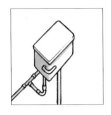 **cistern** A container used to store water.

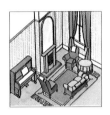 **furniture** Tables, chairs, cupboards and other items that can be moved from room to room.

 **coal** Hard black rock broken into pieces and burnt on a fire.

 **mangle** A metal frame with two or three wooden rollers, used to squeeze the water out of clean, wet washing.

 **copper** A large metal tub. Used to heat water over a fire.

 **scullery** A small room at the back of the house, used for washing clothes and dishes.

 **crib** A small bed with high sides. Used for a baby.

 **soot** Black dust left by smoke from a fire.

 **crockery** Bowls, cups, plates and other pottery objects used for preparing and storing food.

 **utensils** Objects used to prepare and serve food, for example hand whisk, tin-opener, rolling pin.

 **dolly** A wooden stick with three prongs used to stir clothes while they are being washed.

 **worktops** Long flat surfaces in a kitchen, used for preparing food on.

◆ Books to Read ◆

Bathtime by G. Tanner & T. Wood (History Mysteries series, A & C Black, 1993)
Bedtime by G. Tanner & T. Wood (History Mysteries series, A & C Black, 1993)
Cleaning by G. Tanner & T. Wood (History Mysteries series, A & C Black, 1994)
Cooking by G. Tanner & T. Wood (History Mysteries series, A & C Black, 1992)
Cooking by R. Thomson (Changing Times series, Watts Books, 1992)
Housework by G. Tanner (Turn of the Century series, A & C Black, 1992)
In the Home by K. Bryant-Mole (History from Objects series, Wayland, 1993)
Keeping Clean by E. Allen (Turn of the Century series, A & C Black, 1991)
Keeping Clean by K. Bryant-Mole (History from Objects series, Wayland, 1993)
Washday by R. Thomson (Turn of the Century series, A & C Black, 1989)
Washing by G. Tanner & T. Wood (History Mysteries series, A & C Black, 1992)

◆ Places to Visit ◆

Many local museums have small collections of household objects and/or displays depicting the home life of families of different social status. It is worth contacting them to see what they can offer. Historic houses may also provide an experience of how a wealthy family and their servants lived.

Blist Hill Open Air Museum,
Ironbridge, Telford,
Shropshire, TF8 7AW

    Telephone: 0195245 3522

Beamish North of England
    Open Air Museum,
Beamish, County Durham, DH9 0RG

    Telephone: 01207 231811
    Education Officer: Stephen Manion

Castle Museum,
Tower Street, York, YO1 1RY

    Telephone: 011904 653611

Welsh Folk Museum,
St Fagans, Cardiff, CF5 6XB

    Telephone: 01222 569441

The Ulster Folk and Transport Museum,
153 Bangor Road, Cultra Manor,
Holywood, Belfast, BT18 0EU

    Telephone: 012317 5411
    Education Officer: Deirdre Brown

The Tenement House,
    (National Trust – 1890s flat)
145 Buccleuch Street,
Garnet Hill, Glasgow, G3 6QN

    Telephone: 0141 333 0183

· Further Information about the Photographs ·

Terraced house, c.1902.

About this photograph

There was a variety of older and recently built housing in existence at the turn of the century. Newer homes had piped water inside the house. Older properties relied on outside standpipes and in rural areas wells and springs. Electric lighting had been available since the 1880s but was costly and difficult to install. In 1910 only 2 per cent of homes were connected. Gas supplies had been introduced in the 1830s and received a boost from the introduction of the slot meter in 1895. However most homes relied on coal fires for heating and cooking. Oil lamps and candles were the main forms of lighting.

Questions to ask

Why is there a chimney?
Are there houses like this today?

Points to explore

Background – building, materials, features.
People – ages, physical appearance, clothes, pose.

Kitchen, c.1911.

About this photograph

It is difficult to find photographs of 'ordinary' kitchens from this time. In most homes food shopping was done more frequently because goods were perishable and preservation methods expensive and limited.
Also fewer utensils were used so there was less need for storage space.

Questions to ask

What, other than the fire, made this room difficult to clean?
What jobs do you think took place in this room?

Points to explore

Furniture – materials, decoration, function.
Room decoration – patterns, colours, ornaments.

Range, c.1898.

About this photograph

Coal-fired kitchen ranges came in a variety of styles and sizes. This example is from a large house. The open range with the fire box open to the room was most popular in the North but it used a lot of fuel. In the South, the closed range was more frequently used. The fire box was enclosed and the door opened only if the room needed warming. In middle-class homes a servant did the arduous daily cleaning of the fire.

Questions to ask

What is on the range?
Why are there so many pots and pans?
What do you think the shovel was used for?

Points to explore

Kitchen equipment – types, materials, functions.

Wash-day, 1900.

About this photograph

Washing clothes generally took a whole day, with another day spent ironing. Some homes had a wash-house or scullery where the washing was done. On hot days it was preferable to go outside. In smaller homes this was the only option, even in winter. Much of the equipment shown had been in use for 200 years. Washing machines were available but still relied on hand power. They were expensive and by 1914 were only found in about 5 per cent of homes. Electric washing machines were invented in the USA in the 1900s.

Questions to ask

What is the woman doing?
Why is she washing outside?

Points to explore

Background – buildings, materials, features.
Woman – clothing, pose, equipment.

Two maids, c.1910.

About this photograph

Using heated irons for pressing clothes probably originated in China in the 8th century. By the 1900s there were several different types of iron. The box iron had a removable slug which was heated. Some irons had charcoal heated in them. The most popular type of iron was the sad or flat iron shown here. Two irons were needed; one was heated on the range or fire while the other was being used. Electric irons were invented in the 1880s but were very expensive.

Questions to ask

Do the women know the photograph is being taken?
How can you tell?
Why would someone take a photo of ironing?

Points to explore

People – age, gender, clothes, pose.
Equipment – names, materials, function.

Vacuum cleaner demonstration, c.1912.

About this photograph

Carpets and rugs were usually cleaned by hand – hung on a line outside and beaten with a carpet beater. The earliest domestic vacuum cleaner was produced in 1908. The photograph was taken for demonstration purposes. Note the light-coloured walls and fireplace – a result of the introduction of electricity, the 'clean' fuel in newer middle-class homes.

Questions to ask

What is the woman doing?
Do you think this machine was easy to use?

Points to explore

Background – furniture, furnishings, ornaments.
Woman – status, clothes, pose.

PHOTOGRAPH ON PAGE 17

Baby in bath, c.1905.

About this photograph

Photographs of people bathing are difficult to find. We do not know whether the example shown depicts a nanny or mother. Most families used portable tin baths which offered little privacy and required large amounts of water to be heated and carried. Public bath houses were provided in many urban areas. In families with servants, baths were taken in bedrooms. The notion of a separate bathroom emerged in the 1880s and by 1900 some homes with piped water and water heaters had a separate room for bathing. This was seen as a great status symbol.

Questions to ask

Why was the baby bathed in front of the fire?
How often do you think people had baths?

Points to explore

People – age, relationship, pose, clothes.
Room – furniture, decoration, ornaments, heating.

PHOTOGRAPH ON PAGE 19

Privy, c.1920s.

About this photograph

Although the water-closet had been invented in 1589 it was not in general use because it required piped water and a system of sewage pipes to remove waste. Most working class homes had outside earth closets with either a pit or bucket. 'Better' houses had inside toilets – some with separate ones for servants. From the 1920s indoor toilets began to be built in new homes.

Questions to ask

Do you think people liked using an outside toilet?
What might be the problems with an outside toilet?

Points to explore

Buildings – materials, state of repair, decoration.

PHOTOGRAPH ON PAGE 21

Bedroom, c.1907.

About this photograph

The presence of a housekeeper with the mother and baby indicates that this is a middle-class household. Only in wealthier homes would a fire be lit in a bedroom. The furnishings suggest that the baby is sleeping in an adult's bedroom (the parents' or the servant's) rather than a nursery. In poorer families where space was restricted children shared a bedroom (sometimes sleeping 'top to tail' in the same bed) or slept in the same room as their parents. In 1901 40 per cent of families lived in homes of 4 rooms or fewer.

Questions to ask

Who are the people in the photograph?
What are they doing?

Points to explore

People – age, gender, clothes, pose.
Background – furniture, decoration, materials, heating.

PHOTOGRAPH ON PAGE 23

Interior c.1910.

About this photograph

Larger homes had several living rooms (drawing room, dining room, breakfast room, study, library or boudoir). The room shown is from a wealthier home of this type. Note the fresh flowers and the mix of patterns and decorations in the furnishings. Darker colours and patterns were more functional since coal fires and gas lighting were 'dirty' fuels. Even the smallest homes had a room (the front parlour) which was kept for best – despite inconveniencing the family by restricting daily living space.
This idea persisted until the 1950s.

Questions to ask

Would this room be comfortable? Why?
Would this room be easy to keep clean?

Points to explore

Woman – clothes, pose.
Room – heating, lighting.
Background – furniture, ornaments, decorations.

PHOTOGRAPH ON PAGE 25

Family, 1900.

About this photograph

In many working-class homes the kitchen was the centre of family life – also serving as a living room and bathroom. The kitchen was often the only room in the house that was heated so adults and children would spend free time in this room.

Questions to ask

What time of day do you think this is? Why?
Why is the family sitting close to the range?

Points to explore

People – age, gender, pose, clothes, activity.
Background – furniture, decorations, ornaments.

PHOTOGRAPH ON PAGE 27

Family making toys, c.1908.

About this photograph

With few if any labour saving devices, housework was an arduous and long drawn out activity. Yet in poorer families women also had to take on additional paid work to supplement the family income. This work was often home based which meant that child care was not a problem. Home work was poorly paid and frequently required working at night. Where possible other members of the family helped out. In middle-class families 'ladies' did not work. They had servants to carry out all the housework.

Questions to ask

Why is there a bed in this room?
What time of the day do you think it is?
Why are all the family working?

Points to explore

People – age, gender, pose, clothes, activity.
Background – furniture, decorations, ornaments, state of repair.

· Index ·

(Items that appear in text)